How to Dazzle at
Spelling

Irene Yates

Brilliant
PUBLICATIONS

We hope you and your class enjoy using this book. Other books in the series include:

English Titles

How to Dazzle at Grammar	978 1 897675 46 5
How to Dazzle at Writing	978 1 897675 45 8
How to Dazzle at Reading	978 1 897675 44 1
How to Dazzle at Reading for Meaning	978 1 897675 51 9
How to Dazzle at Macbeth	978 1 897675 93 9
How to Dazzle at Twelfth Night	978 1 903853 34 4
How to Dazzle at Romeo and Juliet	978 1 897675 92 2

Maths Titles

How to Dazzle at Oral and Mental Starters	978 1 903853 10 8
How to Dazzle at Algebra	978 1 903853 12 2
How to Dazzle at Written Calculations	978 1 903853 11 5
How to Dazzle at Maths Crosswords (Book 1)	978 1 903853 38 2
How to Dazzle at Maths Crosswords (Book 2)	978 1 903853 39 9

Science Titles

How to Dazzle at Being a Scientist	978 1 897675 52 6
How to Dazzle at Scientific Enquiry	978 1 903853 15 3

Other Titles

How to Dazzle at Beginning Mapskills	978 1 903853 58 0
How to Dazzle at Information Technology	978 1 897675 67 0

To find out more details on any of our resources, please log onto our website:
www.brilliantpublications.co.uk.

Published by Brilliant Publications
Unit 10
Sparrow Hall Farm
Edlesborough
Dunstable
Bedfordshire
LU6 2ES, UK

email: info@brilliantpublications.co.uk
Website: www.brilliantpublications.co.uk

General information enquiries:
Tel: 01525 222292

The name Brilliant Publications and the logo are registered trademarks.

Written by Irene Yates
Illustrated by Michelle Ives

Printed in the UK

© Irene Yates 1998

Printed ISBN: 978-1-897675-47-2
ebook ISBN: 978-0-85747-052-2

First published 1998.
Reprinted 1999 and 2009.
10 9 8 7 6 5 4 3

The right of Irene Yates to be identified as author of this work has been asserted by her in accordance with the Copyright, Designs and Patents Act 1988.

Contents

Introduction

How to Dazzle at Spelling contains 42 photocopiable sheets for use with Key Stage 3 pupils who are working at levels 1-3 of the National Curriculum in English (Scottish levels A-B). The activities are presented in an age-appropriate manner and provide a flexible but structured resource for teaching pupils to understand and commit sounds, letter strings and high-frequency words to memory and, thus, to assist them in developing basic skills.

Because there are so many exceptions to the rules of spelling, they are often difficult for pupils with special needs to assimilate. The rules require reinforcement many times before they are understood. It is only when those rules are fully understood that they become part of the pupils' own abilities in basic skills. Often, pupils appear to have mastered spellings, only to get the words completely wrong when they try to use them in their own writing.

Learning how to spell is not easy for these pupils. Their greatest needs are usually to develop their visual and aural discrimination, visual and aural recognition and their visual and aural memory. They need to have some kind of understanding that if they can *visualize* the words, as well as sound them out, they have a much better chance of spelling them correctly. They also need to have their confidence boosted since they have probably, over their school years, developed an attitude that they will never, ever be able to spell.

Part of the disaffection of pupils with special needs is the misery of failing time after time. The sheets are designed, with information and questioning, to help those pupils to experience success and achievement. The expectation that the pupil *will* achieve will help to build confidence and competence.

The tasks in this book are kept fairly short, to facilitate concentration. The text on the pages is kept to a minimum, and the content of the pages is applied to contexts that the pupils will find motivating. In many cases there is an element of puzzle or competition to the activities to provide greater motivation. The extra task at the bottom of each sheet provides reinforcement and enables pupils to use the skill they have learned in a functional way.

How to use the book

The activity pages are designed to supplement any English language activities you pursue in the classroom. They are intended to add to your pupils' knowledge of how the English language works.

They can be used with individual pupils, pairs or very small groups, as the need arises. The text on the pages has been kept as short as possible, so that reluctant or poorer readers will not feel swamped by 'words on the page'. For the same reason, we have used white space and boxes, to help the pupils to understand the sheets easily, and to give them a measure of independence in working through them. In many instances, a pair of scissors and encouragement to 'cut and paste' may further help the pupils to work through the sheets.

It is not the author's intention that a teacher should expect all the pupils to complete all the sheets, rather that the sheets be used with a flexible approach, so that the book provides a bank of resources that will meet needs as they arise.

Many of the sheets can be modified and extended in very simple ways. The Add-ons can provide a good vehicle for discussion of what has been learned and how it can be applied.

Much of the spelling in this book is related to high-frequency and medium-frequency words so that the pupils can build up a good bank of words that they will need for their own writing. It is advisable to encourage each pupil to make and keep a personal dictionary, one that they feel total ownership of, one that will be a tool for their own success.

The spelling rules, where they have been given, are those which the pupils should be able to follow without too much trouble. The 'i before e' rule has been omitted because it is impossible to write it on a page with enough clarity for special needs pupils to understand it, since it has so many exceptions. Unfortunately, the exceptions would have to be shown on the same page and this would only lead to greater confusion for the pupils. The 'i before e' rule would be much better explained verbally by the teacher.

Spelling trick one

Trick one for learning to spell a word is to do these things – all at the same time!

| look at the word | say it | move your hand to write it |

Try it with these words:

Look and say	Write here
where	
when	
how	
who	
what	
why	
went	
house	
home	
take	
there	
them	
with	

Add-on
Turn this page over and get someone to test you on these words.

Spelling trick two

Trick two for learning how to spell a word is:

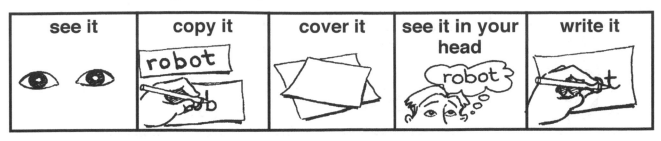

see it	copy it	cover it	see it in your head	write it

So when you look at the word, you try to fix what it looks like in your head.

Try it with these words:

Look	Copy	Cover and imagine	Write
some		⬇	
school		⬇	
does		⬇	
other		⬇	
every		⬇	
first		⬇	
once		⬇	
know		⬇	
half		⬇	
until		⬇	
said		⬇	
friend		⬇	
talk		⬇	

Add-on
Turn this page over and get someone to test you on these words.

Spelling trick three

Trick three for learning how to spell a word is:

look and say	break it into syllables	find the hard bits	give yourself a clue
	di / no / saur	di / no / saur	dino SAUR

For example:

because	be / cause	hard bit is 'cause'	in your head say 'be CAUSE'

Try it with these words:

Look and say	Break into syllables	Find the hard bits	Write
suddenly			
while			
though			
different			
important			
young			
children			
something			

Add-on
Get someone to test you on these words.

Spelling trick four

Trick four for learning how to spell a word is:

look at it	break it into letters	make up a silly sentence or phrase
👁 👁	d o g	Dynamic Old Growler GRR

For example:

earth	e a r t h	Eric always roams the heavens.
goes	g o e s	Go on, end story.
found	f o u n d	Friends often understand nothing doing.

Try it with these words:

Look	Write your sentence here
open	
only	
under	
clothes	
through	
tries	
watch	

Add-on
Get someone to test you on these words.

Vowel sounds

Trace the sounds of the five short vowels with your finger. Say the sound they make. Write a line of each vowel.

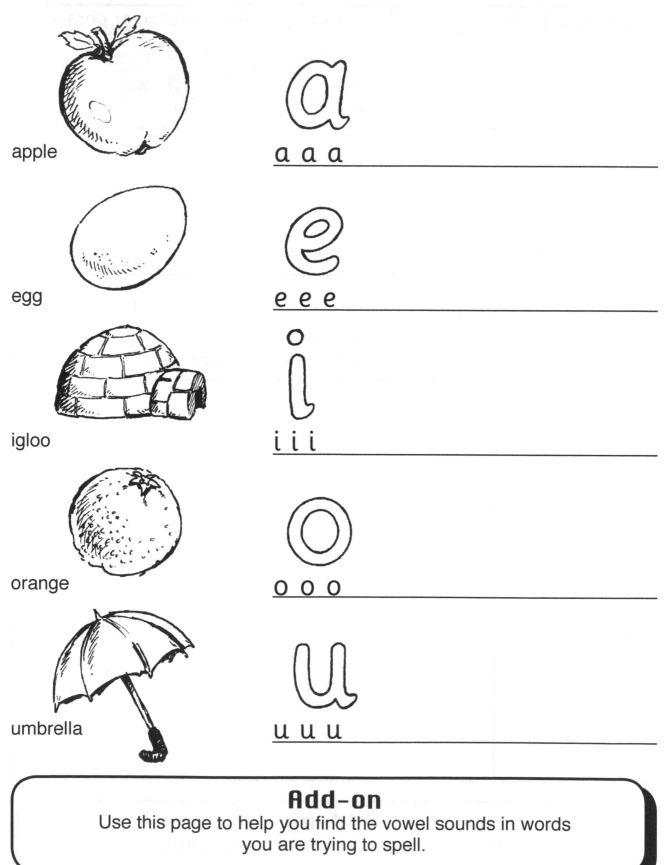

apple

a

a a a _____

egg

e

e e e _____

igloo

i

i i i _____

orange

o

o o o _____

umbrella

u

u u u _____

Add-on

Use this page to help you find the vowel sounds in words
you are trying to spell.

The 'y' factor

Sometimes a 'y' pretends it is a vowel.

'y' acts as a vowel in:

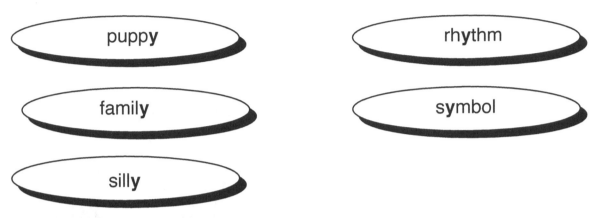

puppy

rhythm

family

symbol

silly

Use a dictionary to find some more words where 'y' acts as a vowel.

Add-on
After you have written the words, check your spelling.

Sound that vowel

These short words all have **short vowel** sounds.

Ben bin ban tin ten top run

Helpline
Only write words with one syllable.

Give yourself ten minutes. Write down as many words as you can for each short vowel.

Add-on
Score two points for each word. Choose six of your words.
Write a sentence for each one.

Long vowels and the silent 'e'

Some vowels are the sounds we hear in:

a	g**a**p	r**a**t
e	p**e**t	th**e**m
i	k**i**t	r**i**p
o	h**o**p	c**o**d
u	**u**s	t**u**b

If you put an 'e' at the end of each of these words, the sound changes:

gap	+	e	=	g**a**pe
pet	+	e	=	P**e**te
kit	+	e	=	k**i**te
hop	+	e	=	h**o**pe
us	+	e	=	**u**se

The vowel sound is now called a long vowel.

Change these short vowel sounds to long vowel sounds by adding an 'e' at the end. Say the new words.

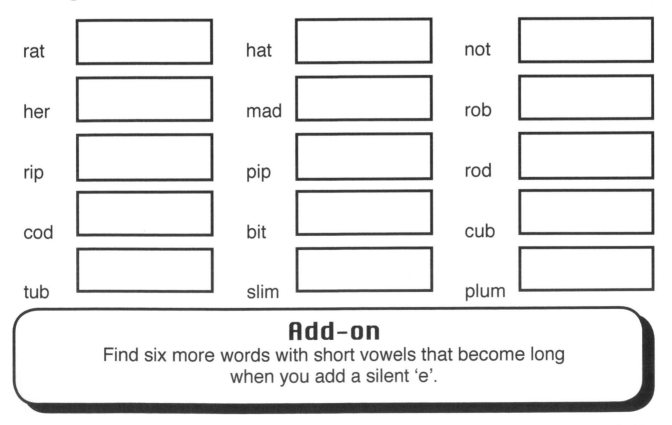

rat		hat		not	
her		mad		rob	
rip		pip		rod	
cod		bit		cub	
tub		slim		plum	

Add-on
Find six more words with short vowels that become long when you add a silent 'e'.

Vowels – short or long?

Remember – a **short vowel** makes its sound as the 'a' in t**a**p or the 'e' in p**e**t.

A **long vowel** says its name, as the 'a' in t**a**pe or the 'e' in P**e**te.

Listen to the word 'battle'. Is the 'a' sound in battle long or short?
What about the 'e' sound in 'nettle'? What about the 'i' sound in 'rifle'?

Say these words. Write them in the correct column.

riddle	bottle	stable	gobble	bugle
struggle	steeple	table	tackle	haggle
paddle	tickle	feeble	rabble	needle

First vowel sound is short	First vowel sound is long

Add-on
Find five more words with short vowels and five words with
long vowels ending with the 'le' sound.

Words with 'ea'

Sometimes 'ea' sounds like 'ee', as in h**ea**r.

Sometimes 'ea' sound like 'e', as in br**ea**d.

Say these words. Write them in the correct column.
Be careful – three of them can go in both columns!

ear   read   bead   tear   lead   instead

tread   head   beak   bear   dear   gear

feather   beam   beach   fear   beaker   clear

real   wear   pear

sounds like hear	sounds like bread

The three words that can go in both columns are:

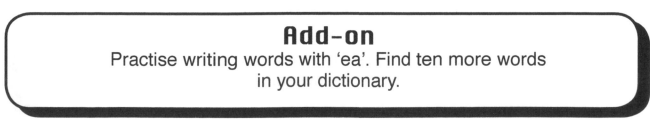

Add-on
Practise writing words with 'ea'. Find ten more words
in your dictionary.

Groups inside

You can find these groups of letters inside many words:

ea   **ee**   **ai**

**Write as many words as you can for each group.
Use a dictionary to help you.**

ea	ee	ai

Add-on
Check your spellings. Try to find words with more
than one syllable.

Ending with a 'y'

Most of the time when you hear an 'ee' sound at the end of a word, the sound is made by writing a 'y'.

For example:

tid**y**   easy peas**y**   cheek**y**

Fill in the words:

#	clue						
1	to be cross	a					
2	lots		m				
3	cheerful	h					
4	idle		l				
5	to apologize	s					
6	plenty to do		b				
7	frightening	s					
8	badly behaved	n					
9	feeling tired	s					
10	with gas or bubbles	f					
11	talks a lot	c	h				
12	nice to look at	p					

Check your spellings.

Helpline
The letter in the tinted box will be a 'y'.

Add-on
Use your dictionary to find, and write out,
ten more words ending with 'y'.

The silent 'e' puzzle

Silent 'e' usually makes a short vowel say its name when there is only one consonant between the short vowel and the 'e'.

For example:

not	+	e	=	not**e**
tub	+	e	=	tub**e**
fin	+	e	=	fin**e**

The 'e' does not have to come at the end of a word to make this happen.

For example: pap**e**r   driv**e**r   mak**e**s

All of the words in the puzzle have an 'e' that changes a short vowel into a long one.

Fill in the puzzle.

#	Clue							
1	You do this with your teeth	b	i					
2	You do this on a bike or a horse	r	i					
3	A feather	p		u				
4	A surgeon does this	o		e		a		
5	Chase someone	p	u			u		
6	Absolute quiet	s	i		e		e	
7	A place to see old things	m	u					
8	Move smoothly	g		i				
9	You do this if you're happy	s		i				
10	Not outside	i			i			
11	A musical instrument	o		o				
12	What we live	l	i					

Add-on
One word in the puzzle fits the rule in one place but not in another. Can you find it?

Consonants

Five of the letters of the alphabet are called **vowels**.
The vowels are **a**, **e**, **i**, **o**, and **u**.

All the other letters of the alphabet are called **consonants**.

Here are the consonants. Fill in the missing vowels.

__	b	c	d	__	f	g	h	__	j	k	l	m
n	__	p	q	r	s	t	__	v	w	x	y	z

Write the letters here:

Vowels

1————
2————
3————
4————
5————

Consonants

1————   8————   15————
2————   9————   16————
3————   10————   17————
4————   11————   18————
5————   12————   19————
6————   13————   20————
7————   14————   21————

Write the whole alphabet here:

a   b ...

Add-on
Say the names of all the consonants in the right order.
Say their sounds in the right order.

Consonant sounds

Here are the consonant letters. Say each letter:

B	C	D	F	G	H	J	K	L	M	N
P	Q	R	S	T	V	W	X	Y	Z	

What sounds do they make? Make each sound:

b	c	d	f	g	h	j	k	l	m	n
p	q	r	s	t	v	w	x	y	z	

Write a word beginning with each of the consonants.

b		p	
c		q	
d		r	
f		s	
g		t	
h		v	
j		w	
k		x	
l		y	
m		z	
n			

Add-on
Write one word *ending* with each of these letters: b, d, g, p and t.

The double consonant puzzle

The words in this puzzle use this rule: after a short vowel sound, double the consonant. The rule works for lots of words (but not for words with a 'k' sound in the middle).

Fill in the puzzle. One word does not fit into this rule.

The word that does not fit into this rule is:

1	A kind of running..................................		j	o						
2	Pulling		t	u						
3	Making a map......................................		m	a						
4	Moaning a lot.......................................		n	a						
5	The jam in a doughnut.........................		f	i						
6	Can't be found.....................................		m	i						
7	Pushing a ball with your toe............	d	r	i						
8	A word for 'man' or 'boy'........................		f	e						
9	A colour..		y	e						
10	Happy..		j	o						
11	A game played with a wooden bat..	c	r	i						
12	Not tidy...		m	e						

Add-on
Choose five of the words and write one sentence for each of them.

The 'ck' puzzle

All of the words in this puzzle have 'ck' after a short vowel sound.

Fill in the puzzle. One word does not have 'ck' in it.

The word that does not have 'ck' is:

1 Use your hand to call someone across to you.................................... | b | e |
2 A team game............................ | b | a | ... | a |
3 You need one of these to be allowed in... | t | i |
4 You can carry water in this.............. | b | u |
5 You put your cash in this.................. | p | o |
6 A kind of lizard................................. | g | e |
7 You plug something into this............. | s | o |
8 An illness... | s | i |
9 Tie something down.................. | s | h | a |
10 A bag you wear on your back........... | r | u | ... | a |
11 A moonship...................................... | r | o |
12 The noise of a clock......................... | t | i | ... | o |

Add-on
Choose five of the words and write one sentence
for each of them.

Syllable patterns

Read these words:

where	after	yesterday	walking
later	tomorrow	when	one
millennium	today	feet	beautiful
speak	afterwards	over	before
somebody	suddenly	ask	

Count how many syllables they have.
Write each word in the correct column.
One word will not fit into any column.

Helpline
You could cut the words out and move them about.

1 syllable	2 syllables	3 syllables

The word that does not fit is:

Add-on
Add three more words to each list. Check your spellings.

Syllables

Words can be broken into **syllables**. Each syllable always has at least one vowel or 'y' in it.

If you remember this, it will help you to spell.

All of the words on this page are about football.

Fit the missing vowels into each syllable.

Words with one syllable:

t __ __ m   pl __ y   g __ __ l

g __ m __   k __ ck   m __ tch

Words with two syllables:

f __ __ tb __ ll   d __ f __ nc __

__ ffs __ d __   wh __ stl __

Words with three syllables:

p __ n __ lt __   g __ __ lk __ __ p __ r

__ tt __ ck __ ng   r __ f __ r __ __

Add-on
Write down any four syllable words you can think of about football.

Patterns in words

Look for the patterns in these words:

quiet	friend	quaint
tearful	aqua	beautiful
field	believe	babble
squire	chief	forgetful
squirt	quickly	brief
artful	sieve	wonderful
thankful		

Helpline
You could cut the words out and move them about.

There are three patterns. Work out what they are and write each word in its column. One word does not fit any column.

Pattern 1 =	Pattern 2 =	Pattern 3 =

The word that does not fit is:

Add-on
Choose two words from each list.
Write one sentence for each word. Check your spellings.

Rule number 1 to remember

This spelling rule is for words of more than one syllable. It works for lots of words (but not for words with a 'k' sound in the middle).

The rule is: After a short vowel sound, double the consonant.

For example: better   supper

                 dinner   follow

                 hopping   sudden

Turn these one-syllable words into new two-syllable words. The first one has been done for you:

Dad ➡ _Daddy_   let ➡_____   sun ➡_____

Mum➡_____   skip ➡_____   swim➡_____

Gran➡_____   pop ➡_____   stop ➡_____

plan ➡_____   big ➡_____   red ➡_____

Find double consonants to finish these words:

po __ __ y   ru __ __ er   si __ __ y

fu __ __ y   ra __ __ it   pe __ __ y

so __ __ y   ye __ __ ow   ha __ __ y

Read the words out loud. Use a highlighter pen to highlight the short vowels before the double consonants.

Add-on
Use your dictionary to find ten more words with a short vowel sound followed by a double consonant.

Rule number 2 to remember

This spelling rule is for words of more than one syllable where the short vowel is followed by a 'k' sound.

The rule is: If you hear a 'k' sound after a short vowel, it is usually 'ck'.

For example: bla**ck**er   be**ck**on

chi**ck**en   po**ck**et

Finish these words:

ja__ __ et   wre __ __ er   ro __ __ et

pa __ __ et   che __ __ ing   lo __ __ et

cra __ __ ing   ki __ __ ing   lu __ __ y

pe __ __ ing   cri __ __ et   clu __ __ ing

**Read the words out loud. Write them out again here.
Use a highlighter pen to highlight the short vowels.**

_____   _____   _____

_____   _____   _____

_____   _____   _____

_____   _____   _____

Add-on
Use your dictionary to find ten more words with a
short vowel sound followed by 'ck'.

The f, l, s spelling rule

Most words of only one syllable that end with 'f', 'l' or 's' have double letters at the end.

For example: cuff   doll   cro**ss**

Fill in the missing words.

1   I __ __ __ __ __   see you tomorrow.

2   __ __ __ __   you be there?

3   Try not to make a   __ __ __ __ .

4   Don't shout or __ __ __ __ .

5   I'll get __ __ __ the bus at the station.

6   This rule will help you to __ __ __ __ __   __ __ __ __ .

7   We go home when the __ __ __ __ rings.

8   Who is in charge? Who is the __ __ __ __ ?

9   __ __ __ __   the ball!

10 The __ __ __ __ __   needs mowing.

Think of some more words of one syllable ending in ff, ll or ss.

ff	ll	ss

Add-on
Learn the words that do not fit this rule. Here are some: of, if, is, us, pal, gas, bus, yes. Can you find any more?

What about the 'c'/'k' sound?

Most times if the hard 'c' sound is followed by **a**, **o**, **u** or a consonant, the 'c' sound is a **c**.

For example: **c**at   a**c**t   **c**ling

Most times if the hard 'c' sound is followed by an **e** or **i**, you need to write a **k**.

For example: **k**ing   **k**ite   du**k**e

Complete these words:

__ at	__ an	__ ut	__ lan	__ een
__ rab	__ od	ra __ e	__ ot	pa __ t
__ ennel	__ itten	__ ind	__ ub	
la __ e	a __ t	bi __ e	awo __ e	

Find ten more words to fit the rule:

c ——————————————   k ——————————————

c ——————————————   k ——————————————

c ——————————————   k ——————————————

c ——————————————   k ——————————————

c ——————————————   k ——————————————

Add-on
Learn the words that do not fit this rule: kangaroo, skate, skull.

Non-stop game

Start with a word.

For example: bear

Your next word has to begin with the last letter of 'bear'.

For example: bear   ➡   red

Your next word has to begin with the last letter of 'red'.

For example: bear   ➡   red   ➡   dirt

Write as many words as you can in ten minutes.

bear ➡ red ➡ dirt ➡ tree ➡ e _____

Don't use the same word twice!

Use a dictionary to help you. Check your spellings.

Add-on
Do the same game but stick to words about a topic, such as animals, games or transport.

The frames game

Your job is to fit in as many words as you can into each of these frames.

Use a dictionary to help you.

Frame 1 r __ __ d	Frame 2 d __ __ r	Frame 3 m __ __ t

Add-on
Turn the last frame round and start again with t __ __ m.

The 'ight' words

Lots of words have the sound 'ite' in them but it is spelled 'ight'. You need to learn these words.

Write 'ight' ten times here:

_____ _____ _____ _____ _____

_____ _____ _____ _____ _____

Read these words out loud:

bright	might	fight	flight	night
right	tight	sight	fright	light

Write one sentence for each of the words.

1 _____

2 _____

3 _____

4 _____

5 _____

6 _____

7 _____

8 _____

9 _____

10_____

Add-on
Make up a word quiz for these words. Get a friend to complete it.
Check your friend's spelling.

The 'ough' words

Lots of words have the letter pattern 'ough' in them. The 'ough' does not always sound the same.

Write 'ough' ten times here:

_____ _____ _____ _____ _____

_____ _____ _____ _____ _____

Do this puzzle. The missing 'ough' word will rhyme with the word in the box.

1   The stone felt __ __ __ __ __ . | stuff |

2   He __ __ __ __ __ __ __ about the match. | caught |

3   The farmer uses a __ __ __ __ __ __ . | cow |

4   We went __ __ __ __ __ __ __ the woods. | to |

5   The pigs had their snouts in the __ __ __ __ __ __. | off |

6   I've had a bad cold and __ __ __ __ __ . | off |

7   The two lads __ __ __ __ __ __ in the street. | taught |

8   The one who won was __ __ __ __ __ . | gruff |

9   You can make some bread from __ __ __ __ __ . | low |

10 I __ __ __ __ __ __ a ticket for the game. | caught |

Add-on
Use your dictionary to find six more words with 'ough' in them.
Practise spelling them.

Could have... should have...

There is one word that people keep getting wrong because they say it in the wrong way.

Often we say, 'could of' or 'should of' when we mean **could have** or **should have**.

Remember: the verbs could, would, will, should and might are *never* followed by the word 'of'. If you hear that sound you *must* use the verb 'have'.

Write two sentences each for:

could have _____

_____

should have _____

_____

would have _____

_____

will have _____

_____

might have _____

_____

Add-on
Make up a silly sentence to help you remember this rule.

Contractions

It's important to know how to spell words that are called **contractions**. Contractions squeeze two words together, lose a letter and put an apostrophe in its place.

For example: do not   =   don't
he is   =   he's

Sometimes you lose more than one letter:

I will   =   I'll

You probably use contractions all the time when you're talking.

Follow the rules to write and spell these:

I am	=	_____	who is	= _____
I have	=	_____	we are	= _____
she is	=	_____	are not	= _____
she will	=	_____	has not	= _____
have not	=	_____	they are	= _____
has not	=	_____	would not	= _____
you have	=	_____	I will	= _____
you are	=	_____	were not	= _____
could not	=	_____	we have	= _____

Add-on
Look in your reading book. Find six more contractions.
Practise spelling them.

Root words

Root words are words which make sense on their own. You can make new words by adding **prefixes** and **suffixes** to root words.

For example:

Prefix	Root word		Suffix		New word
un +	clear			=	**un**clear
	clear	+	ly	=	clear**ly**
	clear	+	ed	=	clear**ed**
	clear	+	ing	=	clear**ing**

Add as many prefixes and suffixes as you can to these words. The words you make must be sensible.

calm
act
sudden
order
do
sleep

Add-on
Write one sentence for each root word.

The prefix 'un'

A **prefix** is a bit which is added at the beginning of a root word to change the word. When you add the prefix 'un' it makes the word mean its opposite.

For example: un   +   happy   =   unhappy

Add 'un' to these words. Write the new words underneath.

certain	beaten	kind
cover	occupied	pleasant
controllable	like	lucky

Write a sentence for each new word. Watch your spelling.

1 _____

2 _____

3 _____

4 _____

5 _____

6 _____

7 _____

8 _____

9 _____

Add-on
Use your dictionary to find six more words with the prefix 'un'.

The prefix 'dis'

A **prefix** is a bit which is added at the beginning of a root word to change the word. When you add the prefix 'dis' it makes the word mean its opposite.

For example: dis   +   content   =   discontent

Add 'dis' to these words. Write the new words underneath.

grace	connect	obey
courage	approve	honest
infect	like	appear

Write a sentence for each new word. Watch your spelling.

1 _____

2 _____

3 _____

4 _____

5 _____

6 _____

7 _____

8 _____

9 _____

Add-on
Use your dictionary to find six more words with the prefix 'dis'.

Words ending in 'ed'

A **suffix** is a bit which is added to the end of a word. Many verbs written in the past tense end in a sound like 't' or 'it'. The sound is spelled 'ed'.

For example: jump**ed**   walk**ed**   jogg**ed**   want**ed**

Write one sentence for each of these verbs. Say the word and watch the spelling carefully.

kicked   _____

helped   _____

wanted   _____

acted   _____

dropped   _____

waited   _____

stopped   _____

thanked   _____

promised   _____

shaped   _____

Add-on
Look in your reading book for ten more verbs ending in 'ed'.
Practise writing them.

The suffix 'tion'

The **suffix** 'tion' sounds like 'shun'. It is *never* spelled shun. Most of the time it is spelled 'tion'.

Keep telling yourself 'tee-ION' spells the sound 'shun'. If you can remember this you will get your spelling right eight and a half times out of ten!

Add 'tion' to these parts of words. Write the words underneath. Say them out loud as you write them.

na _____	igni _____	men _____
opera _____	addi _____	inten _____
mo _____	solu _____	ques _____
por _____	atten _____	inven _____
invita _____	pollu _____	frac _____

Add-on
Look in your dictionary for eight more words ending with 'tion'.

How to Dazzle at Spelling

40   www.brilliantpublications.co.uk

More than one

A **plural** means 'more than one'. To make a word into a plural we usually change the end of the word.

For most words just add an 's'.

For example: dog   ➡   dogs
                 girl   ➡   girls
                 school   ➡   schools

Some words have a hissing sound when you change them to a plural. The sound is made by adding 'es'.

For example: bus   ➡   buses
                 fox   ➡   foxes
                 coach   ➡   coaches

Make these words plural by adding an 's' or 'es'. Write the new words underneath.

snake	day	crisp
home	eye	church
watch	box	scratch
garden	cake	patch

Add-on
Write ten more words that only have an 's' and five that have 'es'.
Check them in your dictionary.

'y' plurals

The rules for words ending with a 'y' are easy.

If there is a vowel before the 'y', add 's'.

For example: valley   ➡   valley**s**

If there is a consonant before the 'y', lose the 'y' and write 'ies'.

For example: ruby   ➡   rub**ies**

Change these words to plurals:

puppy		party	
day		key	
toy		monkey	
boy		curry	
story		cry	
pony		jelly	
family		lady	

Add-on
Choose four of the words. Change them to plurals and
write a sentence for each.

Words ending in 'f'

Words that end with 'f' or 'fe' usually change when you want to turn them into plurals. The 'f' changes to 've' and you have to add an 's'.

For example: loaf   ➡   loa**ves**

               calf   ➡   cal**ves**

Change these words to plurals:

knife   ☐   self   ☐

half   ☐   wife   ☐

shelf   ☐   hoof   ☐

leaf   ☐   scarf   ☐

wolf   ☐   life   ☐

Helpline
Remember! Look, cover, write.

Add-on
Choose five words. Change them to plurals.
Write a sentence for each one. Check your spellings.

Words ending with 'o'

When a word ends with a consonant plus 'o', you usually have to add 'es' to make it plural.

For example: hero ➡ her**oes**

Change these words to plurals:

echo [ ]   cargo [ ]

volcano [ ]   torpedo [ ]

potato [ ]   dodo [ ]

tomato [ ]   tornado [ ]

mosquito [ ]   disco [ ]

dingo [ ]   mango [ ]

Helpline
Remember! Look, cover, write.

Add-on
Choose five words. Change them to plurals.
Write a sentence for each one. Check your spellings.

Can you spell these words?

The missing words in this story are words that we use all the time when we are writing.

Use the words in the word box to fill in the spaces:

On Saturday I [____] into town [____] my friends.

They called [____] me and we got [____] early.

Mum [____] me [____] money to spend.

She [____] me take my little brother. She [____]

he'd got nothing to [____] . I didn't [____] to take him. We

missed the [____] train because he wouldn't hurry

[____] . We all had [____] lunch with us.

My brother [____] me to carry his stuff. At the station we

went [____] the escalator to the shops. That's

[____] I lost him.

Word box			
for	our	first	asked
with	off	went	do
want	some	made	gave
on	said	when	up

Add-on
Write six more sentences for this story on the back of the page.

Learn to spell ...

Practise the words for:

Days of the week – look, cover and write:

Monday	_____	Friday	_____
Tuesday	_____	Saturday	_____
Wednesday	_____	Sunday	_____
Thursday	_____		

Months of the year – look, cover and write:

January	_____	July	_____
February	_____	August	_____
March	_____	September	_____
April	_____	October	_____
May	_____	November	_____
June	_____	December	_____

Numbers – look, cover and write:

one	_____	six	_____
two	_____	seven	_____
three	_____	eight	_____
four	_____	nine	_____
five	_____	ten	_____

Add-on
Find the words in your dictionary for ten different colours and practise writing them.

Check these words, 1

Work with a friend. Both of you look at the lists for five minutes. Try to fix pictures of the words in your head.

Turn over your sheet. Get your friend to read the words in **List one** to you. You write them down on the back of the sheet.

Swap over, and read the words in **List two** to your friend.

List one	List two
about	now
after	once
again	one
another	our
because	out
came	over
could	people
down	saw
from	school
home	should
house	some
how	than
jump	them
laugh	these
little	three
many	took
more	very
must	want
next	what
night	where

Add-on
Swap lists and start again. Check all your spellings.
Score two points for each one you get right.
Learn the ones you get wrong.

Check these words, 2

Work with a friend. Both of you look at the lists for five minutes. Try to fix pictures of the words in your head.

Turn over your sheet. Get your friend to read the words in **List one** to you. You write them down on the back of the sheet.

Swap over, and read the words in **List two** to your friend.

List one	List two
asked	much
began	never
being	often
brought	only
can't	open
change	second
didn't	show
does	sometimes
don't	start
found	still
goes	suddenly
gone	tell
half	today
heard	told
high	tries
I'm	turn
knew	upon
leave	use
might	watch
morning	wake

Add-on
Swap lists and start again. Check all your spellings.
Score two points for each one you get right.
Learn the ones you get wrong.

Lightning Source UK Ltd.
Milton Keynes UK
UKOW07f1806120616

276085UK00003B/71/P